MW00658406

From th

CHARLE

Courageous LEADERSHIP *in a* CORRUPT World

LifeMaps

Insight for Living

COURAGEOUS LEADERSHIP IN A CORRUPT WORLD
A LIFEMAPS BOOK

From the Bible-Teaching Ministry of Charles R. Swindoll

Charles R. Swindoll has devoted his life to the clear, practical teaching and application of God's Word and His grace. A pastor at heart, Chuck has served as senior pastor to congregations in Texas, Massachusetts, and California. He currently pastors Stonebriar Community Church in Frisco, Texas, but Chuck's listening audience extends far beyond a local church body. As a leading program in Christian broadcasting, *Insight for Living* airs in major Christian radio markets around the world, reaching people groups in languages they can understand. Chuck's extensive writing ministry has also served the body of Christ worldwide and his leadership as president and now chancellor of Dallas Theological Seminary has helped prepare and equip a new generation for ministry. Chuck and Cynthia, his partner in life and ministry, have four grown children and ten grandchildren.

Copyright © 2008 by Charles R. Swindoll, Inc.

The introduction was adapted from Charles R. Swindoll's article, "Seven Building Blocks for Leaders," *Insights* (February 2007), 1, 3. Copyright © 2007 by Insight for Living.

Chapter one was adapted from chapter five, "Knocked Down, but Not Knocked Out," in Charles R. Swindoll's book *Hand Me Another Brick: Timeless Lessons on Leadership* (Nashville: W Publishing Group, 2006), 65–77. Copyright © 1978, 1990, 1998, 2006 by Charles R. Swindoll, Inc.

Chapter two was adapted from chapter five, "Knocked Down, but Not Knocked Out," in *Hand Me Another Brick Bible Companion* (Nashville: W Publishing Group, 2006), 47–57. Copyright © 2006 by Charles R. Swindoll, Inc.

Chapter three was adapted from the original outlines and transcript of Charles R. Swindoll's sermon, "The Gathering Storm," from the series *The Majesty of God's Son*. Copyright © 1998, 1999 by Charles R. Swindoll, Inc. In 2008 this series was released into a book, and the title was changed to *Jesus: The Greatest Life of All*. Copyright © 2008 by Charles R. Swindoll, Inc.

Chapter four was adapted from chapter eleven, "The Gathering Storm," in the Bible Companion titled *Jesus: The Greatest Life of All Bible Companion* (Nashville: W Publishing Group, 2007), 101–9. Copyright © 2007 by Charles R. Swindoll, Inc.

All rights reserved worldwide under international copyright conventions. No portion of this LifeMaps book may be reproduced, stored in a retrieval system, or transmitted in any form or by any means—electronic, mechanical, photocopy, recording, or any other—except for brief quotations in printed reviews, without the prior written permission of the publisher. Inquiries should be addressed to Insight for Living, Rights and Permissions, Post Office Box 251007, Plano, Texas, 75025-1007. The Rights and Permissions Department can also be reached at www.insight.org/permissions.

Published By: IFL Publishing House, A Division of Insight for Living
Post Office Box 251007, Plano, Texas 75025-1007

Writer: Michael J. Svigel, Th.M., Ph.D., Dallas Theological Seminary
Editor in Chief: Cynthia Swindoll, President, Insight for Living
Executive Vice President: Wayne Stiles, Th.M., D.Min., Dallas Theological Seminary
Theological Editor: John Adair, Th.M., Ph.D., Dallas Theological Seminary
Content Editor: Amy L. Snedaker, B.A., English, Rhodes College
Copy Editors: Jim Craft, M.A., English, Mississippi College
Melanie Munnell, M.A., Humanities, The University of Texas at Dallas
Project Coordinator, Creative Ministries: Kim Gibbs, Trinity Valley Community College, 1991–1993
Project Coordinator, Communications: Karen Berard, B.A., Mass Communications, Texas State University-San Marcos
Proofreader: Paula McCoy, B.A., English, Texas A&M University-Commerce
Cover Design: Amarilys Henderson, B.F.A., Illustration, Savannah College of Art and Design
Production Artist: Nancy Gustine, B.F.A., Advertising Art, University of North Texas
Cover Image: iStockphoto.com
Inside Cover Image: Insight for Living staff

Unless otherwise identified, Scripture quotations used in this book are from the *New American Standard Bible®* (NASB). Copyright © 1960, 1962, 1963, 1968, 1971, 1972, 1973, 1975, 1977, 1995 by The Lockman Foundation, La Habra, California. Used by permission. All rights reserved. (www.Lockman.org)

Scripture quotations marked (MSG) are from *The Message*. Copyright © 1993, 1994, 1995, 1996, 2000, 2001, 2002 by Eugene H. Peterson. All rights reserved. Used by permission of NavPress Publishing Group.

An effort has been made to locate sources and obtain permission where necessary for the quotations used in this LifeMaps book. In the event of any unintentional omission, a modification will gladly be incorporated in future printings.

ISBN: 978-1-57972-810-6
Printed in the United States of America

Table of Contents

Introduction
Building Blocks of Leadership

In the fast-paced, highly competitive world of the twenty-first century, many of us are overdue for a fresh word from God on leadership. How much we need His steady, unchanging wisdom in our world of Web meetings, sixty-hour workweeks, workplace demands and deadlines, and corporate scandals! It's hard to find a model of godly leadership, isn't it? "How-to" manuals toss us countless tips on getting the job done . . . but few address the *heart* of a leader.

Though projects and people change with every generation, the principles of godly leadership remain the same. The Bible's wisdom may be ancient, but it's never out of date! It continues to speak to those of us in leadership today. Whether you run a business or a home, or serve in ministry, government, education, athletics, or the military, the Bible provides timely and timeless tools for developing godly leadership. These principles shine brightly through numerous Old and New Testament personalities and countless examples of leadership done well. But too few people look to the Bible or turn to God for their leadership training.

As we turn to Scripture, I'm convinced that, with the exception of Jesus Christ, Nehemiah might possibly stand out as the greatest portrait of godly leadership in all of Scripture. In this *LifeMaps* book, we'll have a chance to look more closely at the nitty-gritty leadership of both Christ and Nehemiah. But let's take a moment here at the front to peer over Nehemiah's shoulder and review some commonly overlooked building blocks of godly leadership found in his journal, the book of Nehemiah. As a way of introducing the big picture of leadership and gearing us up for digging deeper into some specifics in this *LifeMaps* book, let's review the things this ancient Jewish leader recorded while rebuilding the wall around Jerusalem. His book is such a treasure trove of leadership insights that its first six chapters should be required reading each year for all those who want to be effective, godly leaders.

The first foundation stone is *a passion for the project*. Passion includes vision, enthusiasm, drive, determination, creative dreams, and innovative ideas. Leaders with passion can grasp the big picture without becoming enmeshed in or preoccupied with all the details. Nehemiah could hardly sleep as he imagined himself accomplishing God's objective (Nehemiah 2:12). His passion was off the chart. Have you evaluated your passion lately?

The second building block is *the ability to motivate others*. Getting along well with others is a crucial part of leadership. This would include such skills as verbalizing ideas, dreams, and concerns; articulating goals succinctly and simply; and demonstrating organizational strength and boundless energy. Leaders who motivate inspire others to do their best. They quickly affirm and remember to give credit where credit is due. Nehemiah was strong at all those points (2:17–18; 3:1–32). Are you a motivator? How might you discover better ways to motivate those under your leadership?

The third stone is *an unswerving confidence in God*. Nehemiah's journal is filled with prayers—silent ones, short ones, specific ones (Nehemiah 1:8–11; 2:4; 4:4–5, 9). He never failed to remind the people of the Lord's presence and protection (2:18, 20). Leaders who are genuinely Christian consistently turn others' attention to the Source of strength—the One who can accomplish the impossible, the awesome Provider. Confidence in Him does not waver. Their faith is contagious. While they may occasionally doubt their own ability, they do not doubt God's invincible commitment to His work. How might you regain confidence in God if you've lost it?

Resilience and patience through opposition mark the fourth piece. Nehemiah endured it all: sarcasm, suspicion, gossip, mockery, threats, anonymous notes, open letters, false accusations—you name it (2:10, 19; 4:1–3, 7–8). None of it moved him. No leader can survive if he or she cannot stay patient and resilient through criticism. It is important to be firm in purpose without becoming cranky, vengeful, defensive, or mean-spirited. Anger expressed for the right reason and at the right time is appropriate and healthy, but holding a grudge is neither. Do you have someone in your life who can refresh you?

The fifth stone to lock in place is *a practical and balanced grip on reality.* While the good leader may have dreams and ideas, he or she doesn't live in a dream world with a fixation on the ideal. The actual facts—the hard pieces of evidence—are in clear focus. As Nehemiah began his opening speech, his pragmatism was obvious to all: "You see the bad situation we are in" (2:17). He told the workers to stay at their jobs, but he wisely stationed others to protect the wall from attack, both praying and taking action (4:9). Smart. Discerning. Tough. He acted without overreacting. He remained gracious yet unbendingly firm. Good leaders maintain that needed balance between being positive and being aware of the negative. Do you have a balanced grip on reality? Or have you set impractical expectations and an unrealistic timeline to achieve them?

Number six is *a willingness to work hard and remain unselfish*. All godly leaders have at least one thing in common: diligence. They also know the value of calling it a day (*diligence* and *workaholism* are not synonyms). Because of his hard work, Nehemiah was "appointed to be their governor in the land of Judah" (Nehemiah 5:14) even before the wall was completed. He accepted his appointment humbly, refusing special treatment and willingly sacrificing for the good of the people (5:15–18). In your own realms of leadership, have you become lazy or self-centered?

Finally, leaders must have *the discipline to finish the job*. Good leaders are finishers. They know how to concentrate on essentials without allowing perfectionistic details to block the path. I am certain that some of the stones in Nehemiah's wall were a tad crooked and a few of the joints may have been loose. Perhaps a gate or two wasn't perfectly level and no doubt a hinge or two squeaked . . . but *that baby got done* (6:15–16). Mission accomplished. The end. *Done!* Do you tend to get distracted by details . . . or derailed by new ideas . . . or bored with the long haul? How can you keep motivated to finish what you've started?

Christian leaders with character continue to be in demand. Ezekiel recorded God's plea for leaders who would "stand in the gap before Me for the land," but, tragically, God "found no one" (Ezekiel 22:30). His search continues today. Let's determine to be the men and women for whom God is searching to close the gap. Let's be the Nehemiahs of this generation—leaders who get things done for God's glory, standing strong on the building blocks of biblical leadership.

In the chapters that follow we will dig into two crucial issues facing godly leaders—handling criticism and facing moral corruption with courage. We will first follow the path of Nehemiah as he rebuilt the walls of Jerusalem, looking closely at his ability to handle destructive criticism with courage and confidence. Then we will bask in the light of the Lord Jesus, who epitomizes leadership integrity by standing strong in the midst of violent storms of opposition.

My hope is that, as you read the material and work through the study and application questions in this *LifeMaps* book, you will become better equipped to handle the inevitable storms of opposition with the calm courage that comes only through Christ.

At its heart, a map is the distillation of the experience of travelers—those who have journeyed in the past and recorded their memories in the form of pictures and symbols. The map represents the cumulative wisdom of generations of travelers, put together for the benefit of those now wishing to make that same journey.

To undertake a journey with a map is therefore to rely on the wisdom of the past. It is to benefit from the hard-won knowledge of those who have explored the unknown and braved danger in order to serve those who will follow in their footsteps. Behind the lines and symbols of the map lie countless personal stories—stories the map itself can never tell. Yet sometimes those stories need to be told, just as the hard-won insights of coping with traveling can encourage, inspire, and assist us.[1]

—Alister E. McGrath

Welcome to *LifeMaps*

On a journey, the important thing is not speed as much as it is *direction*.

But sometimes heading the right way requires some guidance. Think about it. You would never set out on a long road trip without first making sure you knew which direction to go, right? You'd consult a map. For many people, the journey toward a deeper and more meaningful relationship with God lies along new or unfamiliar ground. They need directions; they need a map. And, even with a map, sometimes you can still get lost. When you do, it's the locals who know best—those who have been down the same roads. That's why this book is designed to be completed in concert with someone else. Wise friends or counselors can help encourage us in our spiritual growth and avoid pitfalls along our paths.

Using *LifeMaps*

LifeMaps provides opportunities for individuals to interact with the Bible in different settings and on several levels, depending upon your particular needs or interests. *LifeMaps* also places a tool in the hands of pastors and other Christian leaders, helping them guide others along a journey of spiritual growth through the study and application of the Bible.

For Individuals

You can use *LifeMaps* in your personal devotionals to gain God's perspective on a particular area of Christian living. In addition to offering engaging chapters to read, *LifeMaps* can further your journey of spiritual growth with the help of penetrating questions and opportunities for personal application.

LifeMaps can also serve as a first step to healing or resolving an issue that continues to plague you. Read, reflect, answer the questions, and then contact a competent, mature, godly man or woman to discuss the topic as it relates to your personal situation. This individual can be a pastor, a counselor, or even one of our staff here at Insight for Living in Pastoral Ministries. (See page 67 for information on how to contact Insight for Living.) This step is an essential part of the journey.

For Pastors and Counselors

LifeMaps is designed to guide individuals through an engaging, in-depth study of the Word of God, freeing you to help them apply the truths in even more specific and personal ways. As a vital first step in the counseling process, each volume lays a solid, biblical, theological, and practical foundation upon which you can build. Encouraging individuals to work through the book on their own allows them the time necessary for personal reflection and education while enabling you to target your ministry of personal interaction and discipleship to their particular needs.

For Groups

LifeMaps can serve as a curriculum for home Bible studies, Sunday school classes, and accountability or discipleship groups. Each book in the series contains enough material for group discussion of key questions and noteworthy passages. *LifeMaps* can also foster meaningful interaction for pastors, elders, staff, and Christian leaders during staff devotionals, leadership retreats, or board meetings.

Suggestions for Study

Whether you use *LifeMaps* in a group, in a counseling setting, in the classroom, or for personal study, we trust it will prove to be an invaluable guide as you seek deeper intimacy with God and growth in godliness. In any setting, the following suggestions will make *LifeMaps* more beneficial for you.

- Begin each chapter with prayer, asking God to teach you through His Word and to open your heart to the self-discovery afforded by the questions and text.
- Read the chapters with pen in hand. Underline any thoughts, quotes, or verses that stand out to you. Use the pages provided at the end of each section to record any questions you may have, especially if you plan to meet with others for discussion.
- Have your Bible handy. In chapters two and four, you'll be prompted to read relevant sections of Scripture and answer questions related to the topic.

- As you complete each chapter, close with prayer, asking God to apply the wisdom and principles to your life by His Holy Spirit. Then watch God work! He may bring people and things into your life that will challenge your attitudes and actions. You may gain new insight about the world and your faith. You may find yourself applying this new wisdom in ways you never expected.

May God's Word illumine your path as you begin your journey. We trust that this volume in the *LifeMaps* series will be a trustworthy guide to learning and to your spiritual growth.

Courageous LEADERSHIP *in a* CORRUPT World

Chapter 1

Knocked Down, but Not Knocked Out

The Leadership of Nehemiah

Anyone who steps into the arena of leadership must be prepared to pay a price. True leadership exacts a heavy toll on the whole person—and the more effective the leadership, the higher the price. The leader must soon face the fact that he or she will be the target of critical darts. J. Oswald Sanders wrote:

> No leader is exempt from criticism, and his humility will nowhere be seen more clearly than in the manner in which he accepts and reacts to it.[1]

Unpleasant though it may sound, you haven't really led until you have become familiar with the stinging barbs of the critic. That implies one thing: good leaders must have thick skin.

The Presence of Opposition

Nehemiah had one task, and that was to build a wall around the city of Jerusalem (Nehemiah 2:17). The walls and the city had been destroyed decades earlier, and those Hebrews who remained in the area of Jerusalem dwelled in constant threat of attack from enemies around them. By rebuilding the walls of the city, the Jews who had been scattered for a generation would begin to return to the city in greater numbers. So Nehemiah's task was to lead the people in the mundane task of bricklaying. It doesn't sound very spiritual, but it was God's will for Nehemiah's life.

Called from a prestigious and posh position in the royal court of King Artaxerxes (Nehemiah 1:11; 2:1), Nehemiah had been prepared for the historic building project that would bring new life to the land of his forefathers. In the process of that task, Nehemiah was led by God to appoint workmen for various parts of the project. Some were to build certain gates; some, a section of the wall. Some were to build in the south; others, up north of the city. Everybody had a job to do. The delegation of labor is described in elaborate detail in chapter 3 of the book of Nehemiah.

Shortly thereafter, we read about the opposition that Nehemiah faced while the people of Jerusalem built the wall. God's will didn't allow the project to be completed without opposition. Before the wall was half finished, the sarcastic words of critics bombarded the workers.

> Now it came about that when Sanballat
> heard that we were rebuilding the wall,
> he became furious. (4:1)

What prompted the opposition was the progress in the construction project. One would think that seeing this small band of people succeeding in a massive project would evoke admiration. But this was not so. The heart of the habitual critic resists change. To him or her, change is a threat. In any organization, those who are most critical of change are those who are most inflexible. They resist change, and they become especially suspicious of changes that lead to progress and growth.

It was the change—the growth—that incited Sanballat's anger. Notice also the others involved in the opposition. After Sanballat heard about rebuilding the wall in verse 1, "He spoke in the presence of his brothers and the wealthy men of Samaria. . . . Now Tobiah the Ammonite was near him" (Nehemiah 4:2–3). More often than not, the following is true: critics run with critics. And, obviously, while not all criticism is of the Devil, this criticism was. It was destructive and disturbing.

Every leader must develop the ability to measure the value or worth of criticism. He or she has to determine the source and the motive and must listen with discernment. Sometimes the best course of action is to graciously accept the criticism and learn from it. Other times, it must be strongly resisted.

Nehemiah's critics were constantly in agreement with one another, and their reaction was not a quiet, mildly disinterested one. No, they were angry! They became sarcastic. Look at the sarcasm in verse 3. "Now Tobiah the Ammonite was near [Sanballat] and he said, 'Even what they are building—if a fox should jump on it, he would break their stone wall down!'"

But Tobiah made a crucial mistake because what the people were building was not "their" stone wall. The Lord wanted the wall built. He happened to use Nehemiah as the construction superintendent, but God commissioned the work and owned the final product. Carping critics typically look at situations from a human point of view—*their* walls, *their* plans, *their* comfort, *their* procedure, *their* arrangement—usually wrapping their derision in carefully crafted logic or, even worse, cleverly contorted Scripture. They don't stop to think that they may be criticizing God's project.

People who look at life from the human point of view have problems with projects that require giant steps of faith. As leaders who are Christian, we need to ask ourselves, "Am I really looking to God for vision, for growth, and for direction, or am I taking the easy way out, allowing the status quo to earn approval from my peers and to keep my position secure?" If we earnestly and genuinely seek God's best for our lives, we must learn to keep our eyes open and our attitudes positive—not lacking in discernment but remaining focused and positive. And we must never forget that those who are, by nature, negative and critical will always, *always* be around to create opposition. Nevertheless, the work must go on. Progress should not stop because a loud minority wants to disparage us or hinder the plan.

Facing Criticism Squarely

Let's call this what it is: spiritual warfare. And battles of that sort are best fought from a kneeling position. When those sidewalk supervisors tried to disrupt construction of the Jerusalem wall, Nehemiah responded to the criticism in two significant ways: he prayed and he persisted.

First, *he talked to God about the criticism*. Take note of his unusual prayer.

> Hear, O our God, how we are despised! Return their reproach on their own heads and give them up for plunder in a land of captivity. Do not forgive their iniquity and let not their sin be blotted out before You, for they have demoralized the builders. (Nehemiah 4:4–5)

This is rare! The Bible is filled with "forgive our iniquities," "forgive us our sins," "relieve us of our transgressions," and "cover our transgressions"—but Nehemiah prayed, "*Do not* forgive their iniquity" and "*Let not* their sin be blotted out before You, for they have demoralized the builders" (Nehemiah 4:5, emphasis added). While this may not be a model prayer theologically, I highly commend its honesty!

Please keep in mind that Nehemiah was a great man and a leader we would do well to emulate. He was outraged at the conduct of the critics, and he said some very rash things . . . in the privacy and security of his prayer closet. As we see throughout the book, Nehemiah was a man of prayer (1:4–11; 2:4; 4:4–5; 5:19; 6:14; 13:14, 22, 31). He spent untold hours on his knees, giving vent to his frustrations and his anger, saying to the Lord—in the safety of prayer—what he wanted to say to his critics and to others. Prayer is a great way to unpack our frustrations.

Leaders are often people who have very strong wills. They need this internal drive to overcome the inertia of doubt, fear of change, and criticism. Unfortunately, this quality can make retaliation the most natural response to attack. Building a wall around Jerusalem required someone with Nehemiah's get-tough mind-set. And with opponents like these, it would have been quite understandable if Nehemiah had punched out a few lights. But he didn't go that far.

For the sake of emphasis, let me repeat a very important principle. You are never more successful than when you make your plans, advance your cause, and overcome your obstacles on your knees in prayer. The leader who advances on his or her knees need never retreat. When responding to critics, begin with prayer, then give a response only as the situation compels it.

Proverbs 15:1 says, "A gentle answer turns away wrath, / But a harsh word stirs up anger." What do most of us do when a harsh word is spoken to us? We usually shout louder. Think about your most recent argument. It went on as long as it did because both of you kept adding a comment after the other person. If you want to stop an argument, simply apply Proverbs 15:1 and close your mouth. The other person will usually just run out of gas. If you want to keep the argument going, answer the complaint or criticism in a harsh way. Look at verses 28 and 29 in the same chapter of Proverbs:

> The heart of the righteous ponders how
>   to answer,
> But the mouth of the wicked pours out
>   evil things.
> The LORD is far from the wicked,
> But He hears the prayer of the righteous.
> (Proverbs 15:28–29)

Before Nehemiah said a word to his critics, he talked with his God. He refused to retaliate even though others might have encouraged him to do so. Good for him!

When I was serving the Lord in a church in Waltham, Massachusetts, there was a church in the same area that had an amazing history. One pastor inherited a terrible mess when he first arrived to lead the congregation. Attendance was down, and those who did attend sat in the back three pews. On this pastor's first Sunday, he picked up the pulpit and dragged it down the aisle, placing it near the people. He responded to criticism much the same way, with humor and creativity. With each passing Sunday, the pews filled, forcing him to move the pulpit more and more toward the front of the sanctuary. Before long, he was almost perched in the choir loft! He preached the Word, walked with God, and faithfully labored in spite of opposition. Eventually, God chose to call him to a school that has consistently moved ahead under his guidance.

His successor was a retaliatory man, a fighter. This man held more than one graduate degree; he was absolutely brilliant. He was a well-traveled, well-read, experienced leader of people, seemingly with a lot more going for him than the other fellow. Like his predecessor, this pastor received criticism and hostility from certain segments of the church membership, and week by week—one public argument and retaliatory action after another—the church systematically emptied. Sure, he won the arguments, but he lost the people.

One man fought on his knees, the other on his feet.

Retrain your reflexes. Let your first response to criticism be an honest, cathartic, soul-cleansing season of prayer—take as long as you need. (Let's face it; some of your critics may require you to spend weeks on your knees!) Speak as little in response as you possibly can. Ask the Lord to deal with your critics His way and in His time. Remain focused on your objective. In time, you will find, as I have, that you are never used by God more effectively than when you are praying for your critics.

The Need for Common Sense

Nehemiah's second response to criticism: *he stayed on task*. He persisted. I love what Nehemiah wrote in chapter 4, verse 6: "So we built the wall." The words of criticism fell like rain, yet he continued on. I can just hear him say, in effect: "Keep mixing the mortar and hand me another brick!"

> So we built the wall and the whole wall
> was joined together to half its height,
> for the people had a mind to work.
> (Nehemiah 4:6)

Critics demoralize. Leaders encourage. When the critics spoke, the workmen heard them and were demoralized. But when their leader stepped up and said, "Let's look at it God's way; stay with the job," the crew members were back in there with those trowels and wheelbarrows, putting together the stone and the mortar, building the gates and the hinges.

Nothing excites the opponent or the critic more than his or her negativism hindering the progress of something good. And nothing frustrates him or her more than when we find renewed strength in the Lord to persist. But let's not kid ourselves. Satan won't give up and go away.

Nehemiah said, in effect, "Stay at the task. Don't give up. Keep building." You could hear the workmen day and night, slapping on mortar and setting stones. That productive activity should have assaulted the hearts of Sanballat, Tobiah, and Geshem—but that's not the case. In fact, the size of their group grew. Verses 7 and 8 tell us that Sanballat and Tobiah were joined by the Ammonites and the Ashdodites, and they even added some Arabs. They intensified the opposition. And when they

> heard that the repair of the walls
> of Jerusalem went on, and that the
> breaches began to be closed, they were
> very angry. All of them conspired
> together to come and fight against
> Jerusalem and to cause a disturbance
> in it. (4:7–8)

Sometimes criticism doesn't die down—it intensifies. Not only did the critics expand their troops, but they added intensity to the opposition. They planned a conspiracy and arranged to cause a disturbance. What did Nehemiah do when confronted with continued harassment? As was his custom, he intensified his prayer: "But we prayed to our God, and because of them we set up a guard against them day and night" (Nehemiah 4:9). The intensified opposition might have knocked him down, but it was a long way from knocking him out.

Intensified opposition against the will of God calls for an intensified response. Nehemiah not only heard the opposition but also analyzed available data, prayed, and took decisive, practical action. He set up a guard against them, which was a commonsense response. He persisted by taking up arms.

Occasionally, persistence in the form of common sense must prevail. Do you fear that someone is going to break into your home? Certainly you should trust God, but don't forget to lock the doors. Don't just pray about it. It is foolish to leave doors unlocked when you are praying that your home will not be burglarized.

Out of a job? Pray! But pound the pavement too. Send out the resumé. Make contacts. Pursue as many opportunities as possible. The Lord doesn't have any trouble guiding a moving target. In fact, it's easier to steer a moving vehicle than one that is immobile.

As we close this chapter, don't miss three very practical truths that can be gleaned from Nehemiah 4.

1. *It is impossible to lead anyone without facing opposition.* The leader must learn to take the heat. He or she will face opposition—it's an occupational hazard of every leadership position. Darts will come your way.

2. *It is essential to face opposition with prayer.* The first response to opposition must be prayer. Prayer is the single most often overlooked discipline in the Christian life among leaders.

3. *Prayer is not all that is necessary if opposition grows.* That was true of David. He prayed when Saul was trying to kill him, but he also ran like mad! When opposition intensified, he ran faster. When it got worse, he hid in more obscure places. In many cases, the critic isn't worth the worry. But if the leader has prayed and is still facing intensified opposition, he or she must use common sense.

Many years ago, I became discouraged because of criticism, and my optimism eroded as a lengthy chain of events led me into "the pits." Knowing of my need for encouragement, my wife searched for a way to lift my spirits. She found these encouraging comments written by a statesman I have always admired and gave them to me printed on a wooden decoupage plaque. Consider the words of Theodore Roosevelt:

> It is not the critic who counts; not the man who points out how the strong man stumbles, or where the doer of deeds could have done them better. The credit belongs to the man who is actually in the arena, whose face is marred by dust and sweat and blood; who strives valiantly; who errs, who comes short again and again, because there is no effort without error and shortcoming; but who does actually strive to do the deeds; who knows great enthusiasms, the great devotions; who spends himself in a worthy cause;

> who at the best knows in the end the triumph of high achievement, and who at the worst, if he fails, at least fails while daring greatly.[2]
>
> Far better it is to dare mighty things, to win glorious triumphs, even though checkered by failure, than to take rank with those poor spirits who neither enjoy much nor suffer much, because they live in the gray twilight that knows not victory nor defeat.[3]

I repeat J. Oswald Sanders's statement from the beginning of this chapter: "No leader is exempt from criticism." Don't expect to be. But when it comes, be ready to battle against discouragement, which is poised and ready to strike on the heels of criticism. You can count on it!

My Questions and Thoughts

Chapter 2

Overcoming Criticism

You Are Here

Though all leaders are recipients of criticism, not all criticism is equal. *Constructive* criticism comes from genuine partners in or supporters of a leader's work. Positive critics are motivated by a desire to help, not hinder, the leader. Therefore, they share their concerns in a humble, respectful way. Godly leaders learn to seek out constructive criticism from wise mentors and fellow workers. And they seek to apply their feedback judiciously. Every leader will also quickly become familiar with *destructive* criticism designed to tear down, discredit, and malign.

How can you tell the difference between constructive and destructive criticism? Describe a few characteristics of each as you've experienced them.

Destructive Criticism

Constructive Criticism

Who are your most trusted *constructive* critics?

Using a few short words or phrases, describe their mannerisms, methods, and motives when they offer you constructive criticism.

How do you generally respond to constructive criticism?

Discovering the Way

As soon as Nehemiah and his crew began to rebuild the walls of Jerusalem (Nehemiah 3), opposition and criticism broke out and constantly bombarded them from all sides. In this chapter, we'll dig deeper into some of the passages we looked at in chapter 1 and discover how a leader should handle inevitable criticism in a way that keeps him or her on task . . . and also deepens a leader's walk with God. But first, let's spend a few minutes with a New Testament leader known for his firsthand experience with opposition.

A New Testament Perspective

Of all the New Testament books Paul wrote, 2 Corinthians is one of the most autobiographical. In it Paul provided some honest admissions about ministry, admitting both his human frailty and his absolute dependence on God's power working within him.

Read 2 Corinthians 4:7–10.

God is not only interested in blessing a humble "clay pot," He is also interested in using the vessel itself as an object lesson in godliness. He puts the truth in a human life and then places that life in front of an audience, whether it's a Bible-study group of five or a professional corporation of five thousand. He uses regular individuals to *display*, not just contain, the glory of God.

Paul's words in 2 Corinthians 4:8–10 contain an implicit promise . . . but not the kind we like to hear: opposition is inevitable. And yet, to counter the discouragement that follows such a promise comes radiant, God-given hope: We may be knocked down, but we're not knocked out!

In your current realms of leadership, who are your toughest *destructive* critics or opponents?

____

____

____

____

____

____

Using a few short words or phrases, describe their mannerisms, methods, and motives when they assault you with destructive criticism.

____

____

____

____

____

____

How have you handled their attacks in the past? By avoiding, ignoring, defending, or fighting back? Why do you think you tend to respond in this way?

The Old Testament Example of Nehemiah

As the scene opens on Nehemiah 4, the wall has gotten off to a good start. Then, enter Sanballat and Tobiah: critics extraordinaire. As the wall grew daily, their irritation escalated. The signs of progress and growth incited them to sarcastic opposition. Like most habitual critics, they felt threatened by the thought of change and saw it as something to be resisted.

Read Nehemiah 4:1–3.

Notice that the conversation in Nehemiah 4:1–3 was one-sided. It did not contain one ounce of balanced perspective. One man's comments incited similar comments from another. How typical! As we have seen, critics often associate with other critics. They like to be around people who will reinforce their views.

What types of critical comments are the most difficult for you to hear? Give a few recent examples.

What is it about these remarks that makes them linger in your mind?

Every group—including every church or ministry—has its Sanballats and Tobiahs. They are unavoidable. So how do we handle them? Let's look at Nehemiah's response to negative, destructive criticism.

Often our first reaction to criticism is a quick retort. But Nehemiah kept his cool. *His first response was to talk to God.*

Read Nehemiah 4:4–5.

We can tell from Nehemiah's requests that he felt like retaliating. But instead of striking back, he spent some therapeutic time on his knees, bringing his concerns before God. It takes two to argue, but an argument dies on the spot if one person refuses to participate. And it's the words that fly thoughtlessly off our tongues that we regret later, not the ones that have been pondered in secret before the Lord.

Read Proverbs 15:1, 28. Practically speaking, how did Nehemiah's response illustrate the principles found in these verses?

Have you ever made prayer your first response when you experienced criticism? What effect did it have on the situation? On you?

Notice a second thing about Nehemiah's response to Sanballat's and Tobiah's criticisms—*he stayed at the task.*

Read Nehemiah 4:6.

Critics demoralize; leaders encourage. We know from Nehemiah 4:5 that Sanballat's and Tobiah's barbs had pricked a hole in the people's enthusiasm, but Nehemiah kept them focused on the task and encouraged them to work with renewed determination. We can imagine him standing up after his time of prayer and shouting, "Keep pouring that mortar! Bring on those stones! Keep going, and God's going to help us build this wall!"

Nothing riles critics more than having their criticism result in further progress. The sight of those Jews slathering on that mortar and hauling in those stones made Sanballat and his cohorts more furious than ever. So, instead of backing off, they strengthened their attack.

Doorway to History

Money, Money, Money

Have you ever wondered why Sanballat and the wealthy men of Samaria so vigorously opposed Nehemiah's work? Was it religious bias, racial prejudice, or personal resentment? The answer might be simpler than these: *money*.

Though we cannot dismiss the religious and cultural differences that caused conflict at that time, Sanballat's response to the building project seems to have been motivated by a fear of loss. He could lose his prevailing share in the market, eventually losing money and power. A fortified Jerusalem meant Sanballat's monopoly in the region would be challenged. When the pocketbooks of the powerful are threatened, they often pull out all the stops to protect their positions.

Not much has changed, has it? In today's world of business, academics, politics—and, sad to say, even ministry—economics motivates much of the opposition, positioning, and fighting. Because every endeavor depends on the availability of finances, discouragement can easily turn to pressure, stress, and strain and give rise to all kinds of arguments and backbiting.

Read Nehemiah 4:7–9.

Though the critics conspired to unleash a full-blown frontal assault, Nehemiah wouldn't stand for defeat. Yet for all his determination, he didn't try to take matters into his own hands. He matched intensified opposition with intensified prayer, this time bringing his workers with him to the throne of God (Nehemiah 4:9). Nehemiah thought practically as well as prudently. He brought his frustration to God, and he also took action.

What steps have you taken to shield yourself and those who depend on your leadership from the painful effects of destructive criticism? If you have not done anything, consider what steps you could take.

Starting Your Journey

Criticism can be demoralizing, discouraging, and incite us to do or say things we later regret. We've all been there, and we will be again. But what worked in Nehemiah's situation centuries ago can work just as well in our lives today. Let's revisit three very practical truths from Nehemiah 4 mentioned in the previous chapter.

First, *realize that it is impossible to lead without facing criticism*. Whether you're the CEO of a Fortune 500 company or the president of the PTA, if you lead, you will hear complaints from jealous and jeering outsiders or competitors. You can count on it. And if you don't actually hear them, you might as well assume somebody is criticizing you in private. So refuse to view criticism as a sign of failure; recognize it as a part of the fallen world we live in.

Second, *it is essential that your first response to opposition is prayer.* There's no better place to cool your anger and gain perspective on your actions than on your knees. Once again, Nehemiah illustrated this principle well.

Third, *prayer may not be all that is necessary if opposition intensifies*. If you notice a fire blazing in your kitchen, you need to pray for God to save you, but you also need to reach for the fire extinguisher! God gave us minds and bodies so that we may take practical action when it's needed. Prayer should always be the preface to action.

When it comes right down to it, the barbs of carping critics and pesky pessimists are usually not worth the worry they cause. Every project and leader has its adversaries. When appropriate, listen to their comments to determine if what they have to say has any validity. But if you detect the singsong ring of a lifelong naysayer, follow Nehemiah's example: don't let it rattle you, and don't let it hinder the work God has given you to do. Criticism may knock you down, but don't let it knock you out!

When you're being harangued by criticism, take some time to think through the following questions.

How does this particular criticism make you feel? Hurt, angry, or frightened? What does the Bible say about how to deal with these emotions? (To find specific verses on emotions such as anger, fear, or anxiety, you may wish to consult a Bible concordance. One can be found online, at a library, or often in the back of your Bible.)

What major or minor issues does the criticism really focus on? Are these legitimate concerns? Why, or why not?

Do you perceive that ulterior motives might be driving the critic, such as pride, jealousy, hurt/pain, cynicism, stubbornness, or greed? If so, how should you gauge your response?

After pondering these questions thoroughly, address each one with God in prayer. With Nehemiah's example in mind, formulate a wise, appropriate response to the criticism you face—a response that will keep you focused on the leadership task God has called you to complete. Write your prayer below.

Leaders will face criticism. It is inevitable and unavoidable. While we can learn from constructive criticism, destructive criticism can be demoralizing, debilitating, and distracting. But through prayer and a wise response, we can keep the task in front of us and our people with us. Has criticism knocked you to the ground? While you're there, spend time with God in prayer, and then get up and go. As it does to all leaders, criticism will occasionally knock you down . . . but it doesn't have to knock you out.

My Questions and Thoughts

My Questions and Thoughts

Chapter 3

The Gathering Storm

Leadership Lessons of Jesus

Among the treasured books in my library is a six-volume set by Winston Churchill that covers the transition of time during the Second World War—not only during the war but preparing people for the war. In fact, his first volume is dedicated to the whole idea of how that war came to be. He titled that volume, appropriately, *The Gathering Storm*.

Churchill set the scene after the First World War when "peace" was on everybody's lips. They danced in the streets, rejoicing with the soldiers and sailors who were returning from that war. And people were walking around with the idea that it was over, the worst was behind them, the best was yet to come . . . that World War I was the war to end all wars.

But Churchill paused in the midst of this celebration to remind everyone that broken and defeated Germany was already in the process of rearming. What appeared to be the end of something terrible was a time to regroup for something even worse.

History teaches us something about life today. While politicians seek to restore peace, promise a better economy, and push for positive change, it's difficult not to imagine that behind the public hype a storm is gathering.

Navigation through the unexpected storms requires leadership that stands strong for the truth—even if it means stepping on toes.

The Gathering Storm around Jesus's Ministry

When we look at Jesus's ministry, it's easy to see how people around Him would have been thinking, *What a leader!* He filled their stomachs with food, healed their diseases, and promised a kingdom where they would be free to worship their God. And all the while, during those dreamy moments when many people were hoping for the best, there was at the same time a plan to put Jesus to death.

Now, if you weren't familiar with the story, you would never guess this plan was led by religious people. The whole idea of putting a man like Jesus on a cross, driving spikes into His hands and feet, dropping that timber into a hole, and leaving Him there to die sounds a lot like something a bunch of polytheistic Romans would concoct. But in reality the plot to destroy Jesus began in the hearts of men who had been deeply embarrassed by Him and His teaching. They were hypocritical men who liked to be noticed in the public places and liked to be seen for their long robes and long prayers and impressive appearances. They were the religious and political leaders of the Jews—the Sadducees, the scribes, and the Pharisees. And Jesus was making them mad.

I find it interesting that in Matthew 10 Jesus counters any people-pleasing notions as He states the mission of His life in just a handful of shocking words.

> "Do not think that I came to bring peace on the earth; I did not come to bring peace, but a sword. For I came to set a man against his father, and a daughter against her mother, and a daughter-in-law against her mother-in-law; and a man's enemies will be the members of his household." (Matthew 10:34–36)

Jesus didn't say we should stop honoring and appreciating our parents and family. He was simply saying that when it comes to the maximum loyalty, it must first go to Christ and none other. That's tough teaching, but it's often the price for taking a stand for the truth. Jesus remembered His mission in the midst of conflict.

Now let's look at an example of how audacious Jesus's leadership looked in the eyes of His opponents. His critics came from Jerusalem, their headquarters—traveling north to Galilee in order to confront Jesus regarding His policies, procedures, and personnel. This was a tense moment. The cloud of opposition was gathering on the horizon, and the storm was coming.

> Then some Pharisees and scribes came to Jesus from Jerusalem and said, "Why do Your disciples break the tradition of the elders? For they do not wash their hands when they eat bread." And He answered and said to them, "Why do you yourselves transgress the commandment of God for the sake of your tradition?" (15:1–3)

To appreciate this confrontation, you have to understand a couple of things. First, Jesus pointed out the difference between the tradition of the Jewish elders and the commandment of God. We understand the commandment of God would be the Mosaic law, known among the Jews as the Torah—Genesis through Deuteronomy, the books of Moses, the written Word of God, not to be tampered with, only to be obeyed. But in those days, the Pharisees and the religious leaders had added to the laws of Moses things that God Himself had not commanded. Second, to those men, obeying the traditions was just as important as obeying the commandments of God. In the process of a growing tradition, they gave equal responsibility to their rules and traditions as they did to the Mosaic law. They had established an elaborate system of holy hand-washing, to be performed both before, after, and during the meal. God didn't require it . . . *they* required it. And so they saw the disciples, hungry as they were, plucking and eating some of the grain as they followed their Rabbi. Of course, the disciples didn't wash their hands as the tradition required. So the Pharisees asked, "Why do Your disciples not obey our traditions?"

Jesus looked these religious prudes in the eye and answered, in effect, "You have invalidated the Word of God by changing it." Look at what He said:

> "For God said, 'Honor your father and mother,' and, 'He who speaks evil of father or mother is to be put to death.' But you say, 'Whoever says to his father or mother, "Whatever I have that would help you has been given to God," he is not to honor his father or his mother.' And by this you invalidated the word of God for the sake of your tradition." (Matthew 15:4–6)

And if that wasn't embarrassing enough for these Pharisees, Jesus then quoted from Isaiah and applied the message to them:

> "You hypocrites, rightly did Isaiah prophesy of you: 'This people honors Me with their lips, but their heart is far away from Me. But in vain do they worship Me, teaching as doctrines the precepts of men.'" (Matthew 15:7–9)

Talk about courageous leadership! When was the last time you had the courage to call anybody the "h" word? Probably never . . . at least not to his or her face. Jesus stood straight and called it like it was. The sword of truth has but one target: the heart. And when the heart of a hypocrite is pierced, it bleeds resentment . . . and, ultimately, hatred.

That's exactly the reaction we see from these opponents. I have a little smiling face written in my Bible alongside verse 12. When you read it, you'll understand why: "Then the disciples came and said to Him, 'Do You know that the Pharisees were offended when they heard this statement?'" (15:12).

Do you think Jesus cared that the Pharisees were offended? Of course not! If standing for the truth sometimes means putting a wedge between family relationships, it certainly means offending hypocritical opponents. This applies to leadership across the board. I don't know that we ever carried out discipline with our children that didn't offend them at the moment. I don't think that I have ever been reproved correctly until there has been a moment of offense that gets my attention.

I hope you're beginning to see the backbone of our Lord. The false image of Jesus as *only* gentle, meek, mild, and quiet has affected us long enough. That's not His leadership style. He didn't just stand back, let things happen, and accept everybody no matter what. Yes,

He was gentle, He was meek, He was humble of heart, He was gracious and forgiving and understanding and accepting. But when He encountered wrong, when He came to the place where compromise would betray the truth of God, He called it what it was: hypocrisy.

As we jump forward in these events leading up to Jesus's arrest, we see the clouds of opposition thickening and the thunder of criticism rumbling. Note how the Lord handled it. He saw the war growing and intensifying. He was never ignorant of the enemy's presence. When opposition was growing, albeit hidden, it was exposed to Him. And when push came to shove, He spoke as few have ever spoken. He wasn't worried about being politically correct. He didn't concern Himself with what His opponents thought of Him. He stood before His God and was able to say at the end, "I have done what You sent Me to do." He never lost sight of His mission, regardless of who it offended, regardless of what it meant for Him personally. That's great leadership.

We see another example of Christ's bold leadership in Luke 19, when Jesus cleansed the temple. Please understand the setting. In those days there was a gathering held regularly called the Annas Bazaar—established by the former high priest and his mafia-like family to control the lucrative temple worship. The bazaar lined the family's pockets and funded their corrupt hold on power. The chief priests only accepted shekels minted in Israel, so money changers within the temple precincts gladly exchanged any currency for Jewish shekels at an inflated rate and then pocketed the difference. On top of this, the law of Moses stated that any animal offered to God had to be flawless, so the priests inspected the animals brought for sacrifice and arbitrarily rejected animals so they could offer a suitable replacement for a fee. Ironically, the "suitable" animal sold to the unsuspecting worshiper had, only moments before, been the rejected sacrifice of a previous worshiper!

The Annas Bazaar had the word *scam* written all over it. The temple that had been designed for prayer had been turned into a marketplace of deceit. Jesus walked into the midst of this scene and His righteous anger moved Him to act.

> Jesus entered the temple and began to drive out those who were selling, saying to them, "It is written, 'And My house shall be a house of prayer,' but you have made it a robbers' den."
> (Luke 19:45–46)

Can you imagine the scene? In all the images I've ever seen of Jesus, He looks half-alive and half-dead, sort of like a monk in pain, leaning against something or stooped over. But Luke 19 shows us Jesus with a whip, throwing chairs and tables, pushing the animals, driving the people out of the temple. While many of the people were attracted to His decisive leadership, His uncompromising resolve, and His principled life, the illegitimate leaders of Israel felt threatened:

> "He was teaching daily in the temple; but the chief priests and the scribes and the leading men among the people were trying to destroy Him" (19:47).

Things occur the same way today. A few generations ago, while all the world was calling World War I the war to end all wars, Adolf Hitler engineered his insidious plans to rearm and rise again. The same is true in every realm of leadership today. There is a war on—even if you can't see it! The plot to put Jesus to death was not made in an announcement over some public address system. The conspiracy against Christ developed behind closed doors, in the religious headquarters where evil often lurks, where many don't think clearly or biblically . . . but often politically and selfishly.

But Jesus's leadership among the people kept frustrating His opponents' plans: "They could not find anything that they might do, for all the people were hanging on to every word He said" (Luke 19:48). Those hypocrites had a problem on their hands. The general public thought, *Finally somebody is willing to take a stand . . . call it like it is . . . bring about real change! That's leadership!*

In a fine little book called *Jesus CEO*, Laurie Beth Jones writes:

> Jesus did not mumble or whisper his message. He did not discuss for hours the safest approach for doing something. He did not go through countless committees to get permission to make a statement. He was bold.
>
> He shouted. He stomped. He flung tables and chairs. He cried. He groaned. Everything he did made a statement about what he saw his mission to be. He crashed into people's consciousness with deeds, attitudes, and actions that had never been done, seen, or even heard of before. One could say he used his very blood to paint his message. That was how bold he was.[1]

Did you realize you were following someone that dangerous when you decided to follow Jesus? Did you know He stood defiantly in the face of wrong?

Sometimes the Jesus we seek to imitate looks nothing like the Jesus of the Bible. If you enjoy sitting in the background, letting evil lurk and run its course, saying nothing and doing nothing, you're part of the problem, not part of the answer.

Now I realize that these are also dangerous words and easy to misunderstand and misapply. I want to warn you against making explosive action a habit of your life. Jesus didn't weave a whip together every other week. When some people read messages like this they decide to take on the whole world. They become very difficult to be around. I'm not talking about cultivating a conspiracy mentality. I'm not saying that every evil deed needs to be publicly addressed and every hypocrite needs to be instantly confronted face to face. I'm saying that sometimes a Christlike leader needs to say and do things that will shake up the status quo. If not, the wicked rearm, and battles will be won by the wrong side.

I'm especially concerned about this issue because I keep an eye on politics and hear the latest polls. And I wonder when character, integrity, and true leadership took a vacation. Too few are the individuals willing to stand up and say, "I don't know about you, and I may be the only one in this organization willing to say it, *but this is wrong!*" Not enough are willing to stand for what they know to be the truth in their government . . . at their schools . . . in their neighborhoods . . . in their businesses. Stand alone and stand strong! Christ is your model.

Jesus, on more than a few occasions, used such words as *be aware*, *wake up*, *warn your children*, *instruct them*, *prepare yourself*. The enemy is working. Anything worth cultivating for the good of God and the glory of Christ is going to be assaulted by the enemy. Whether you see it or not, a war is on!

Let's take a look at one more passage; then, I want to apply these leadership lessons directly.

> Now during the day [Jesus] was teaching in the temple, but at evening He would go out and spend the night on the mount that is called Olivet. And all the people would get up early in the morning to come to Him in the temple to listen to Him. Now the Feast of Unleavened Bread, which is called the Passover, was approaching. The chief priests and the scribes were seeking how they might put Him to death; for they were afraid of the people.
> (Luke 21:37–22:2)

The chapter break between Luke 21 and 22 hides the intended contrast. It looked as though everybody was following Christ's lead, and if you could have asked the average shopkeeper along the main street of Jerusalem what he thought about Jesus, you probably would have heard this kind of answer: "Oh, everybody's following Him. He's the most popular preacher around. It's unbelievable. Look at the crowds! Every morning they're up early, hanging on His every word." But they would have been wrong. Not everybody was enamored with Jesus's bold leadership. The conspiracy of priests, scribes, and Pharisees sought how to put Jesus to death.

Get it straight, men and women. There's a war on. Opposition is lurking. Assaults are ready. Don't be lulled to sleep by the good times and the few easy, dreamy vacation moments of today.

Let me apply all of this to where we are. I have four principles I'd like to share. I want you to keep these in mind as you lead a family, a ministry, a business, or even a nation. I want you to remember that some things call for courage.

First, *remembering your mission helps you navigate through the storm*. This will keep you focused. Jesus said, "Do not think that I came to bring peace on the earth; I did not come to bring peace, but a sword" (Matthew 10:34). Whenever you think with discernment, you've added a sword to your life that divides. But in our unfocused, sloppy-thinking era, it's very easy to believe the lie, to go with the crowd.

Second, *encountering evil often requires sword-like confrontation*. This will help you stay alert. Have you ever been around parents who didn't believe in discipline but preferred to keep their kids happy? They'd cave in to every demand of their children. Sometimes strong words of confrontation are like sword thrusts. Imagine if Jesus had casually walked into the temple court, folded His arms, and said, "Now people, this is no way to treat the house of worship, is it?" Do you think they would have listened? But when He pulled out a whip, He got their attention. Sometimes leadership calls for a whip.

Third, *being bold when there's a principle worth fighting for is worth the risk*. This helps you stay courageous. Some will be offended by this. But that's the price leaders must be willing to pay. One of the reasons I admire Winston Churchill as much as I do is because this little, pudgy, cigar-smoking leader had the courage to call Hitler what he was—a demented Austrian corporal. While most were saluting that godless dictator, Churchill called him what he was: a man of prejudice and evil. The peacemakers and compromisers never bent Churchill's will. Are you like that when you have to be? I'm not saying we need to live our whole lives like that. But when you need to be, are you? Even if it means your job?

Fourth, *speaking up for what is right is no guarantee you'll win or be respected*. This will keep you realistic. Most leaders in this world do not operate according to God's rules. This is why truth-tellers often find themselves on the receiving end of the most outrageous abuse imaginable. So be realistic, but take courage. Your stand on truth may not be vindicated anytime soon or even in your lifetime. However, a two-fisted grip on the sword of truth, while sacrificial, does offer great reward. It grants freedom from guilt and shame. It nurtures contentment, instills confidence, stimulates creativity, fosters intimacy with God and others, inspires courage, and sets people free. And we have His promise that He will amply reward any sacrifice that truth demands, if not in this life, then certainly in the life to come.

My Questions and Thoughts

My Questions and Thoughts

Chapter 4

Surviving the Storm of Compromise

You Are Here

When people pursue leadership development, they often put time, money, and effort into becoming more influential, more efficient, and better users of finances, resources, and personnel. Comparatively less time is spent on honing moral leadership, issues such as integrity, honesty, squaring off against wrong, and standing up for what's right.

Yet if Christ is to be our model leader, we cannot ignore His character and moral leadership.

Sadly, people often portray Jesus only as a meek and mild leader who taught His followers to love others as themselves, to avoid retaliation by turning the other cheek, to pursue peace, and to avoid judging others. In many people's minds, that's the perfect picture of a servant-leader—much more "servant" than "leader." While Jesus did indeed possess these qualities and teach these values, the picture is incomplete. Jesus was more than the pale, languid figure often portrayed in art, on television, and in movies.

How would you describe your own style as it relates to moral leadership in your realm of influence? Do you tend to be diplomatic, hands-off, or even passive? Or are you more assertive, active, or even pushy?

Recall a time when you should have shown patience and diplomacy but erred by tactlessly tackling an issue or problem.

Recall a time when you needed to assertively pursue an issue but rather fell into passivity.

Which approach—aggressive or passive—is more Christlike? Explain your answer.

Discovering the Way

We've all encountered the image of a passive, lamb-like Jesus in books, media, or even sermons. While Jesus was indeed gentle and kind, He also took a bold stand against sin. In fact, when confronting evil dressed in the garb of religion, His formidable anger took many by surprise. He sharply rebuked the religious leaders in Israel for turning their privileged status into an opportunity to gain wealth and power. And from the example of Jesus, we learn how to stand up for the truth, even if we lose popularity and suffer persecution for doing what is right.

Read Matthew 15:1–14.

What complaint did the religious authorities have against Jesus and His disciples?

What authority did Jesus say the Pharisees and scribes had defied?

Doorway to History

The Roots of Ritual

Many centuries before the earthly ministry of Jesus, the Jewish people were conquered by the Babylonians and carried off to Babylon as slaves. With their temple destroyed and their homeland colonized by other cultures, the Jews looked to the law of Moses to sustain their national identity and to maintain their distinctiveness as God's chosen people.

In order to help them apply the Law to everyday life in their new and unfamiliar home, teachers of the Jewish Scriptures wrote very careful, specific instructions for the people to follow.

However, what began as a practical aid for contentious Jews became a sacred tradition that took on a life of its own. For instance, ceremonial washing of the hands became an end in itself. Stone water jars were kept ready for use before every meal. A special glass measure was used to draw a small amount from the jars, just enough to fill about one and a half eggshells. The water was first poured on both hands, the fingers pointing upward, as it flowed over the wrists. If the water stopped short of the wrists, the hands remained unclean. And if it ran down the fingers again, the hands became unclean again for the water was now itself unclean. Next, each hand was cleansed by being rubbed with the fist of the other.[1] A very devout Jew would undertake this process not only before a meal but also between each of the courses of the meal.

The body of sacred traditions developed by "the elders" eventually supplanted the very Law it was intended to uphold. And by the time of Jesus, failure to observe tradition was regarded as disobedience to the Law of God. Furthermore, this man-made religiosity became the means by which many Pharisees maintained the illusion of moral superiority over others. Ironically, their religious zeal put them at odds with God. Not only were they motivated by a lust for power, their traditions often violated the very Law they supposedly cherished.

God is not impressed by religious fervor or hollow adherence to rules. He wants people to do what is right because they are motivated by love for Him.

Jesus applied the words of the prophet Isaiah when speaking to the religious leaders in Matthew 15:7–9. What was His opinion of the religious practices?

____

____

____

____

____

Why do you think the disciples were afraid after the encounter? Describe Jesus's attitude.

____

____

____

____

____

Later in His ministry, Jesus publicly condemned the religious system in Jerusalem and exposed the moral bankruptcy of the men who ran it.

Read Matthew 23:1–12.

What do you think could have motivated the religious leaders to behave as they did?

Was Jesus guilty of inciting the people to revolution? Why, or why not? What did He tell them to do?

Read Matthew 23:13–33.

Jesus punctuated each count of His indictment against the crooked religious leaders with a "woe," and then He addressed the scribes and Pharisees directly.

To what disparaging images did Jesus liken the hypocritical religious leaders?

How would you describe Jesus's emotions in this event? Use several one-word descriptions.

As we learned in the previous chapter, during the time of Jesus's earthly ministry, sacrificial worship in the Jerusalem temple had become big business for religious leaders. Moneychangers within the temple precincts gladly exchanged any currency for Jewish shekels at an inflated rate and then pocketed the difference. Furthermore, they arbitrarily rejected animals so that they could offer a suitable replacement sacrifice in exchange for a fee.

Read Luke 19:45–48; 21:37–22:2.

How did Jesus address the abuse taking place in the temple?

Considering the actions and attitudes of the religious leaders, do you think Jesus's response was appropriate? Why, or why not?

Even though Jesus knew the storm was brewing and that His actions would provoke the leaders to anger, why do you think He continued to act so forcefully?

____

____

____

____

____

____

If you were in Jesus's situation, what reasons might you give for not ousting the moneychangers completely or for not sticking around to teach in the temple afterward (Luke 19:47)?

____

____

____

____

____

While Jesus had a soft spot in His heart for people who had been trampled by the world's system, He had little patience for those in religious leadership who neglected or abused others. They had direct access to the truth of God, yet they used their privileged position to hoard wealth and power. Make no mistake; they knew what they were doing. And when Jesus boldly exposed their rebellion, it put Him on a collision course with evil.

What do you find surprising about the portrait of Jesus's leadership in these passages?

What do you find refreshing?

Starting Your Journey

Obviously, not every encounter with wrong-doing should be met with such outrage and passion. Jesus encountered evil in many different forms, and He often responded with compassion for the sinner. Nevertheless, even when Jesus took a more gentle approach, He was always fearless and direct.

Describe a current situation in which you feel you should take a stand against something you know to be wrong.

What is the morally correct choice?

What opposition or consequences will you face if you stand up for what is right?

Is taking a stand worth it? Why, or why not? What reasons might you give for avoiding confrontation?

As we determine to take our own stand against wrong, we can learn from four principles that emerge from the example of Jesus's leadership.

First, *remembering your mission helps you navigate through any storm. Stay focused.* It's not enough to know what's wrong with a situation; we must also define what is right. Once we have determined the correct course of action, we must then keep our eyes focused on following it, even if others discourage or persecute us.

Jesus recognized that His mission was to do His Father's will and that it would not always be popular (Matthew 10:34; 26:39). How would you define your personal mission as it relates to godly leadership?

Other than Jesus, name someone who championed right in the face of wrong, despite great personal suffering or sacrifice. For what or whom did he or she fight, and what was the result?

Next, *encountering evil requires sword-like confrontation, not peacekeeping compromise. Stay alert.* One early Christian writer likened God's Word to a "two-edged sword . . . able to judge the thoughts and intentions of the heart" (Hebrews 4:12). In other words, God's truth has a way of cutting to the heart of a matter. When a clear moral issue is at stake, people-pleasing compromise will tempt us to lay aside the truth of God's Word. However, we must remember to keep our sword pointed at the issue and be willing to take action.

In the specific situation you listed on page 49, what do you think would happen if you compromised your moral stand in order to gain the approval of others?

____

____

____

____

____

____

Third, *being bold when there's a principle worth fighting for is worth the risk, even if it offends and results in misunderstanding. Stay strong.* Misunderstanding is the occupational hazard of leadership. Others will certainly misunderstand or even deliberately misconstrue your intentions, cutting to the heart of your (and every person's) basic desire to be liked. Nevertheless, the moral stand you take will be, ultimately, worth the sacrifice, as you reap the rewards of a life pleasing to God (Luke 6:23–24; Colossians 3:23–24).

Other than Jesus, name a historical figure who weathered the storm of criticism for the sake of his or her moral stand. How has history judged him or her as a result?

Finally, *speaking up for what is right is no guarantee you'll win or gain respect. Stay realistic.* Jesus took a strong stand against the outrageous evil of the religious leaders in Jerusalem and a storm quickly gathered around Him. He understood the risk. In fact, He knew it would lead to His death. He said to the disciples on the eve of His arrest,

> "If I hadn't come and told [the religious leaders] all this in plain language, it wouldn't be so bad. As it is, they have no excuse. Hate me, hate my Father—it's all the same. If I hadn't done what I have done among them, works no one has *ever* done, they wouldn't be to blame. But they saw the God-signs and hated anyway, both me and my Father. Interesting—they have verified the truth of their own Scriptures where it is written, 'They hated me for no good reason.'"
> (John 15:22–25 MSG)

Sometimes the evil we face is so firmly entrenched that we will not see its defeat in our lifetime. In fact, the fight may even require us to sacrifice everything, including our lives. But the Lord does not call us to be successful. He calls us to be faithful. Success or failure is ultimately His responsibility. Ours is to be sure we stand on the correct side of the issue.

When faced with taking a stand for what is right, our greatest temptation is to remain neutral, to forfeit moral leadership for the sake of popularity. Certainly, we should choose our battles wisely and be sure of our motives before we take a stand. But we cannot allow the approval of others to outweigh faithfulness to God and the truth He loves so much. Like Jesus, we must stand up for the truth, even if we lose popularity and suffer persecution for doing what is right.

My Questions and Thoughts

My Questions and Thoughts

How to Begin a Relationship with God

The Bible is the most marvelous book in the world, and it is the true Life-Map that marks the path to God. This map tells us not only how to avoid pitfalls and how to navigate the sudden roadblocks in life, but it also reveals how to enjoy the journey to the fullest. How? It points us to God—our ultimate destination. It tells us how we can come to know God Himself intimately. Let's look at four vital truths the Scripture reveals.

Our Spiritual Condition: Totally Corrupt

The first truth is rather personal. One look in the mirror of Scripture, and our human condition becomes painfully clear:

> There is none righteous, not even one;
> There is none who understands,
> There is none who seeks for God;
> All have turned aside, together they
> have become useless;
> There is none who does good,
> There is not even one.
> (Romans 3:10–12)

We are all sinners through and through—totally corrupt. Now, that doesn't mean we've committed every atrocity known to humankind. We're not as *bad* as we can be, just as *bad off* as we can be. Sin colors all our thoughts, motives, words, and actions.

Look around. Everything around us bears the smudge marks of our sinful nature. Despite our best efforts to create a perfect world, crime statistics continue to soar, divorce rates keep climbing, and families keep crumbling.

Something has gone terribly wrong in our society and in ourselves, something deadly. Contrary to how the world would repackage it, "me first" living doesn't equal rugged individuality and freedom; it equals death. As Paul said in his letter to the Romans, "The wages of sin is death" (Romans 6:23)—our emotional and physical death through sin's destructiveness, and our spiritual death from God's righteous judgment of our sin. This brings us to the second truth: God's character.

God's Character: Infinitely Holy

How can God judge each of us for a sinful state we were born into? Our total depravity is only half the answer. The other half is God's infinite holiness.

The fact that we know things are not as they should be points us to a standard of goodness beyond ourselves. Our sense of injustice in life on this side of eternity implies a perfect standard of justice beyond our reality. That standard and source is God Himself. And God's standard of holiness contrasts starkly with our sinful condition.

Scripture says that "God is Light, and in Him there is no darkness at all" (1 John 1:5). He is absolutely holy—which creates a problem for us. If He is so pure, how can we who are so impure relate to Him?

Perhaps we could try being better people, try to tilt the balance in favor of our good deeds, or seek out wisdom and knowledge for self-improvement. Throughout history, people have attempted to live up to God's standard by keeping the Ten Commandments or living by their own code of ethics. Unfortunately, no one can come close to satisfying the demands of God's law. Romans 3:20 says, "By the works of the Law no flesh will be justified in His sight; for through the Law comes the knowledge of sin."

Our Need: A Substitute

So here we are, sinners by nature and sinners by choice, trying to pull ourselves up by our own bootstraps and attain a relationship with our holy Creator. But every time we try, we fall flat on our faces. We can't live a good enough life to make up for our sin, because God's standard isn't "good enough"—it's *perfection*. And we can't make amends for the offense our sin has created without dying for it.

Who can get us out of this mess?

If someone could live perfectly, honoring God's law, and would bear sin's death penalty for us—in our place—then we would be saved from our predicament. But is there such a person? Thankfully, yes!

Meet your substitute—*Jesus Christ*. He is the One who took death's place for you!

> [God] made [Jesus Christ] who knew no sin to be sin on our behalf, so that we might become the righteousness of God in Him. (2 Corinthians 5:21)

God's Provision: A Savior

God rescued us by sending His Son, Jesus, to die for our sins on the cross (1 John 4:9–10). Jesus was fully human and fully divine (John 1:1, 18), a truth that ensures His understanding of our weaknesses, His power to forgive, and His ability to bridge the gap between God and us (Romans 5:6–11). In short, we are "justified as a gift by His grace through the redemption which is in Christ Jesus" (3:24). Two words in this verse bear further explanation: *justified* and *redemption*.

Justification is God's act of mercy, in which He declares believing sinners righteous, while they are still in their sinning state. Justification doesn't mean that God *makes* us righteous, so that we never sin again, rather that He *declares* us righteous—much like a judge pardons a guilty criminal. Because Jesus took our sin upon Himself and suffered our judgment on the cross, God forgives our debt and proclaims us PARDONED.

Redemption is Christ's act of paying the price to release us from sin's bondage. God sent His Son to bear His wrath for all of our sins—past, present, and future (Romans 3:24–26; 2 Corinthians 5:21). In humble obedience, Christ willingly endured the shame of the cross for your sake (Mark 10:45; Romans 5:6–8; Philippians 2:8). Christ's death satisfied God's righteous demands. He no longer holds your sins against you, because His own Son paid the penalty for them. You are freed from the slave market of death, never to be a slave again!

Placing Your Faith in Christ

These four truths describe how God has provided a way to Himself through Jesus Christ. Because the price has been paid in full by God, we must respond to His free gift of eternal life in total faith and confidence in Him to save us. We must step forward into the relationship with God that He has prepared for us—not by doing good works or by being a good person, but by coming to Him just as we are and accepting His justification and redemption by faith.

> For by grace you have been saved through faith; and that not of yourselves, it is the gift of God; not as a result of works, so that no one may boast. (Ephesians 2:8–9)

We accept God's gift of salvation simply by placing our faith in Christ alone for the forgiveness of our sins. Would you like to enter a relationship with your Creator by trusting in Christ as your Savior? If so, here's a simple prayer you can use to express your faith:

> *Dear God,*
>
> *I know that my sin has put a barrier between You and me. Thank You for sending Your Son, Jesus, to die in my place. I trust in Jesus alone to forgive my sins, and I accept His gift of eternal life. I ask Jesus to be my personal Savior and the Lord of my life. Thank You. In Jesus's name I pray, Amen.*

If you've prayed this prayer or one like it and you wish to find out more about knowing God and His plan for you in the Bible, contact us at Insight for Living. You can speak to one of our pastors or women's counselors on staff by calling 972-473-5097. Or you may send a letter to the address below.

Insight for Living
Pastoral Ministries
Post Office Box 269000
Plano, Texas 75026-9000
USA
www.insight.org/contactapastor

The next time you study a road map, remember the One who created the perfect plan for your life, and remind yourself that you know Him personally. Rejoice in His indescribable gift!

Endnotes

Opening Quote

1. Alister E. McGrath, *The Journey: A Pilgrim in the Lands of the Spirit*, 1st ed. (New York: Doubleday, 2000), 21–22.

Chapter 1

1. J. Oswald Sanders, *Spiritual Leadership*, rev. ed. (Chicago: Moody Press, 1980), 177.
2. Theodore Roosevelt, "The Man in the Arena: Citizenship in a Republic" (address, delivered at the Sorbonne, Paris, April 23, 1910), http://www.theodoreroosevelt.org/research/speech%20arena.htm (accessed August 12, 2008).
3. Theodore Roosevelt, "The Strenuous Life" (speech, delivered to the Hamilton Club, Chicago, April 10, 1899), http://www.theodoreroosevelt.org/research/speech%20strenuous.htm (accessed August 12, 2008).

Chapter 3

1. Laurie Beth Jones, *Jesus, CEO: Using Ancient Wisdom for Visionary Leadership* (New York: Hyperion, 1995), 113.

Chapter 4

1. Alfred Edersheim, *The Life and Times of Jesus the Messiah*, vol. 2 (Grand Rapids: Eerdmans, 1962), 11.

Resources for Probing Further

Resources by Charles R. Swindoll and Insight for Living

Over the years, Chuck Swindoll and the staff at Insight for Living have produced a number of biblical, practical guides to help develop godly leadership. The following are available from Insight for Living by contacting the Insight for Living office near you. See "Ordering Information" beginning on page 69 for contact details.

Swindoll, Charles R. *Hand Me Another Brick: Timeless Lessons on Leadership*. Nashville: W Publishing, 2006. Bible Companion with study and discussion questions also available.

Swindoll, Charles R. *So, You Want to Be Like Christ? Eight Essentials to Get You There*. Nashville: W Publishing, 2005. Workbook for individuals or small groups also available.

Insight for Living. *Character Counts: Building a Life That Pleases God Bible Companion*. Plano, Tex.: IFL Publishing House, 2008.

Suggested Resources by Other Authors

For further help in enhancing your own leadership qualities, here are a few resources we'd like to suggest.

Of course, we cannot always endorse everything a writer or ministry says, so we encourage you to approach these and all other extra-biblical resources with wisdom and discernment.

Barna, George. *Leaders on Leadership: Wisdom, Advice, and Encouragement on the Art of Leading God's People*. Ventura, Calif.: Regal, 1997.

Barna, George. *The Power of Team Leadership: Finding Strength in Shared Responsibility*. Colorado Springs: WaterBrook, 2001.

Blue, Ron, with Jeremy White. *The New Master Your Money: A Step-by-Step Plan for Gaining and Enjoying Financial Freedom*. Chicago: Moody Publishers, 2004.

Finzel, Hans. *The Top Ten Mistakes Leaders Make*. Colorado Springs: David C. Cook, 2007.

Gangel, Kenneth O. *Feeding & Leading: A Practical Handbook on Administration in Churches and Christian Organizations*. Grand Rapids: Baker Books, 2000.

Malphurs, Aubrey. *Being Leaders: The Nature of Authentic Christian Leadership*. Grand Rapids: Baker Books, 2003.

Malphurs, Aubrey. *Values-Driven Leadership: Discovering and Developing Your Core Values for Ministry*. 2d ed. Grand Rapids: Baker Books, 2004.

Sande, Ken. *The Peacemaker: A Biblical Guide to Resolving Personal Conflict*. 3d ed. Grand Rapids: Baker Books, 2004.

Sanders, J. Oswald. *Spiritual Leadership: Principles of Excellence for Every Believer*. Rev. ed. Chicago: Moody Publishers, 1994.

Swenson, Richard A. *Margin: Restoring Emotional, Physical, Financial, and Time Reserves to Overloaded Lives*. Rev. ed. Colorado Springs: NavPress, 2004.

We Are Here for You

If you desire to find out more about knowing God and His plan for you in the Bible, contact us. Insight for Living provides staff pastors who are available for free written correspondence or phone consultation. These seminary-trained and seasoned counselors have years of experience and are well-qualified guides for your spiritual journey.

Please feel welcome to contact your regional Pastoral Ministries by using the information below:

United States

Insight for Living
Pastoral Ministries
Post Office Box 269000
Plano, Texas 75026-9000
USA
972-473-5097, Monday through Friday,
8:00 a.m. – 5:00 p.m. Central time
www.insight.org/contactapastor

Canada

Insight for Living Canada
Pastoral Ministries
Post Office Box 2510
Vancouver, BC V6B 3W7
CANADA
1-800-663-7639
info@insightforliving.ca

Australia, New Zealand, and South Pacific

Insight for Living Australia
Pastoral Care
Post Office Box 1011
Bayswater, VIC 3153
AUSTRALIA
1 300 467 444

United Kingdom and Europe

Insight for Living United Kingdom
Pastoral Care
Post Office Box 348
Leatherhead
KT22 2DS
UNITED KINGDOM
0800 915 9364
+44 (0) 1372 370 055
pastoralcare@insightforliving.org.uk

Ordering Information

If you would like to order additional *LifeMaps* or other Insight for Living resources, please contact the office that serves you.

United States

Insight for Living
Post Office Box 269000
Plano, Texas 75026-9000
USA
1-800-772-8888
Monday through Friday,
7:00 a.m. – 7:00 p.m.
Central time
www.insight.org
www.insightworld.org

Australia, New Zealand, and South Pacific

Insight for Living Australia
Post Office Box 1011
Bayswater, VIC 3153
AUSTRALIA
1 300 467 444
www.insight.asn.au

Canada

Insight for Living Canada
Post Office Box 2510
Vancouver, BC V6B 3W7
CANADA
1-800-663-7639
www.insightforliving.ca

United Kingdom and Europe

Insight for Living United Kingdom
Post Office Box 348
Leatherhead
KT22 2DS
UNITED KINGDOM
0800 915 9364
www.insightforliving.org.uk

Other International Locations

International constituents may contact the U.S. office through our Web site (www.insightworld.org), mail queries, or by calling +1-972-473-5136.